YUMMY! WHAT & WHY?
Healthy Foods for Kids
Nutrition Edition

BABY PROFESSOR

EDUCATION KIDS

Speedy Publishing LLC
40 E. Main St. #1156
Newark, DE 19711
www.speedypublishing.com

Healthy foods are the food we eat that keeps us well and lets us be physically active. They also help protect our body from sickness. Eating the right kind of food means we get all the right nutrients that our body needs.

What are nutrients?

Nutrients are the substances in food that our bodies need in order to work. The essential nutrients your body needs are determined by your age, growth stage and level of activity.

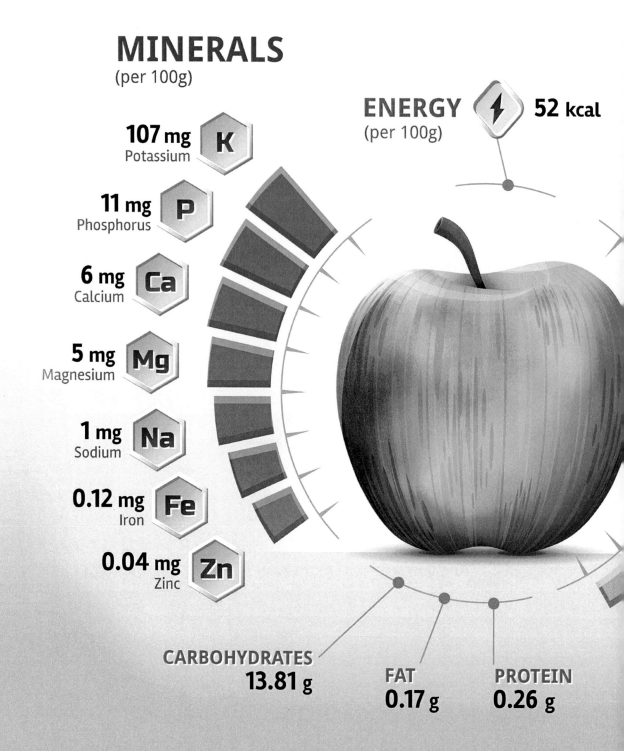

MINERALS
(per 100g)

107 mg — **K** — Potassium

11 mg — **P** — Phosphorus

6 mg — **Ca** — Calcium

5 mg — **Mg** — Magnesium

1 mg — **Na** — Sodium

0.12 mg — **Fe** — Iron

0.04 mg — **Zn** — Zinc

ENERGY
(per 100g)

52 kcal

CARBOHYDRATES
13.81 g

FAT
0.17 g

PROTEIN
0.26 g

VITAMINS
(per 100g)

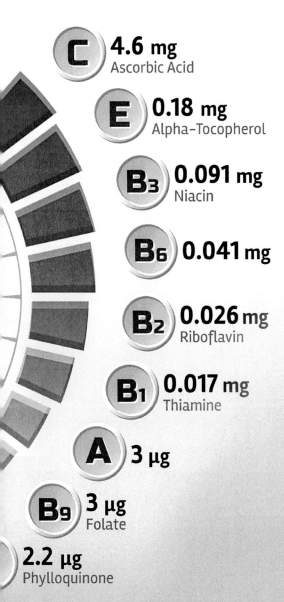

C **4.6** mg
Ascorbic Acid

E **0.18** mg
Alpha-Tocopherol

B₃ **0.091** mg
Niacin

B₆ **0.041** mg

B₂ **0.026** mg
Riboflavin

B₁ **0.017** mg
Thiamine

A 3 µg

B₉ 3 µg
Folate

2.2 µg
Phylloquinone

Nutrients are so tiny that they can't be seen by the naked eye. Nutrients are mostly set into two categories: macronutrients such as carbohydrates, protein, and fats; micronutrients like vitamins and minerals such as calcium, iron, vitamin C.

The key to healthy eating is to enjoy a variety of nutritious foods from several food groups. If you eat a variety of foods, your body will receive all the nutrients and vitamins it needs to function.

Shown here are different food groups on a plate, in the proportion that you should be eating each day. It is important that you get the right amount of each food group in your diet.

Fruit and Veggies

Fruit provides vitamins, minerals, dietary fiber and nutrients naturally present in plants that help your body stay healthy.

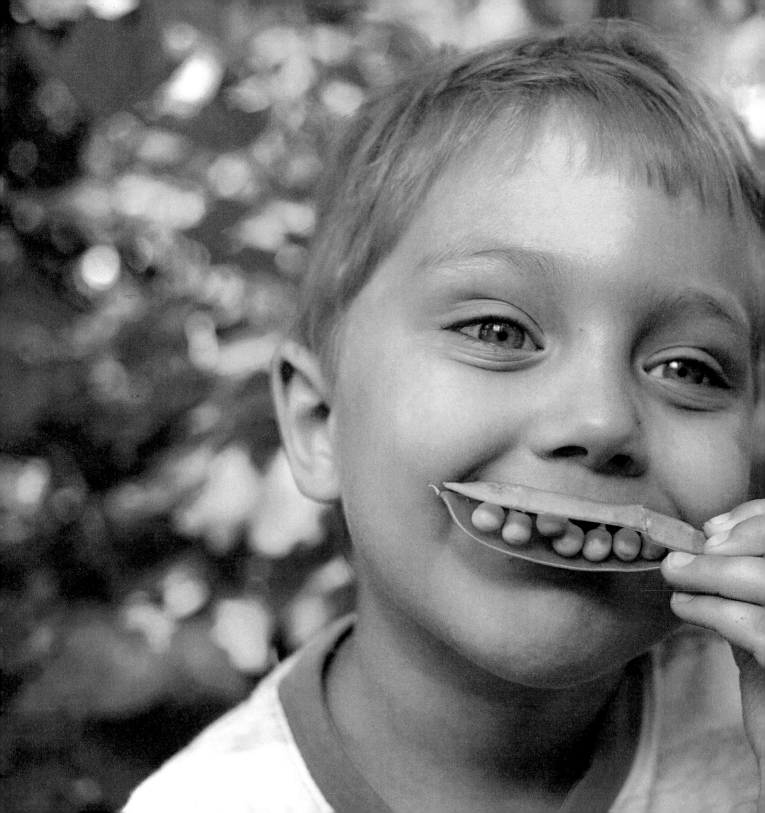

Vegetables should make up a large part of your daily meal and should be recommended at every meal including snacks. They provide vitamins, minerals and dietary fibers to keep your body stay healthy.

Dairy

Dairy products like cheese, milk and yogurt give children the best needed nourishment. They provide calcium, vitamins A and B12, and are one of the best sources for protein.

Try to avoid too many flavored yogurts as these can be high in sugar. Choose natural or Greek varieties instead.

Grains (cereals)

Always choose whole grain varieties as these provide more fiber and nutrients.

They also provide slow energy flow which will keep children fuller and energized for a long period of time.

Protein

Proteins consist of lean meats, poultry, eggs, nuts, seeds and tofu. Our body takes the protein we eat to make specialized chemicals such as hemoglobin and adrenaline.

Protein also builds, maintains, and fixes the tissues in our body. Organs like your heart and muscles are made of protein.

Fats and Sugar

Fats are important for children, but in moderation. The healthy fats are monounsaturated and polyunsaturated. It can be found in nuts, seeds, avocados and oily fish. Other saturated fats are found in pastries,

animal fats and baked goods. They often have poor quality and comes with a lot of sugar and salt. These types of foods should be kept as special treats. Too much sugar can damage children's energy, ruins teeth and cause obesity.

Salt

Adults shouldn't exceed 6 grams a day; children should have less. As a general guide, kids aged 4 to 11 should have between 3-6 grams a day.

Start looking at food labels and remember that many processed foods contain lots of salt.

Drinks

Drinks in between meals, the best drinks to choose in between meals are water and milk. Both are kind to the teeth.

Drinks with sugar like fruit juice and carbonated drinks should be enjoyed as a treat and with meals to control damage of teeth.

Healthy eating for kids starts with breakfast. Children who enjoy breakfast every day have improved memories, good mood and energy, and get higher scores at school.

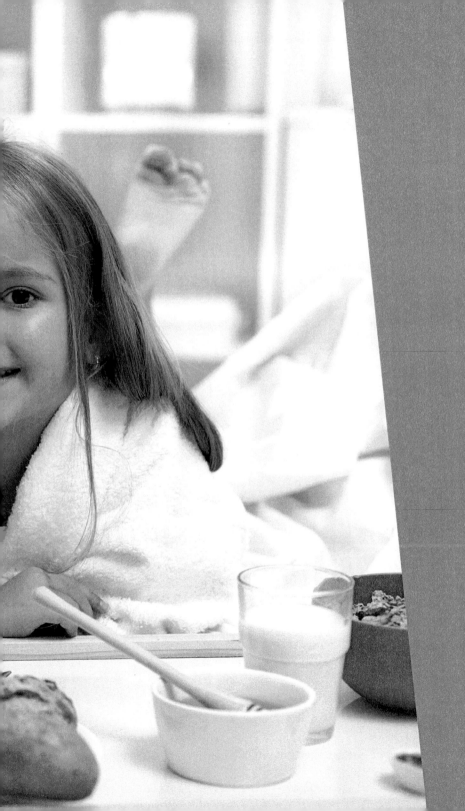

Eating a breakfast high in quality protein from enriched eggs, cereal, cheese, yogurt, milk, meat, or fish can even help lose weight.

A nutritious snack is important to help keep your child's energy levels consistent and their appetite satisfied! Sweet slices of fruit with unsweetened nuts, butter, or natural yogurt with mango or papaya are perfect for a healthy snack.

A child's body gets all the sugar it needs from what exists naturally in food. Added sugar makes a lot of empty calories that causes hyperactivity, mood disorders, risks for obesity and even diabetes.

Fast food is typically high in sugar, unhealthy fat and calories and low in nutrients.

Still, junk food is tempting, so instead of eliminating it entirely, you can try to substitute healthier alternatives.

Skip the fries.
As a substitute,
take along a bag
of tiny carrots,
grapes, or other
fruits and
vegetables.

Trans fats are found in vegetable shortening, fried foods, candies, cookies, snack foods, baked goods, and other processed foods made with somewhat inorganic vegetable oils. Some claim to be trans-fat-free but these claims are false.

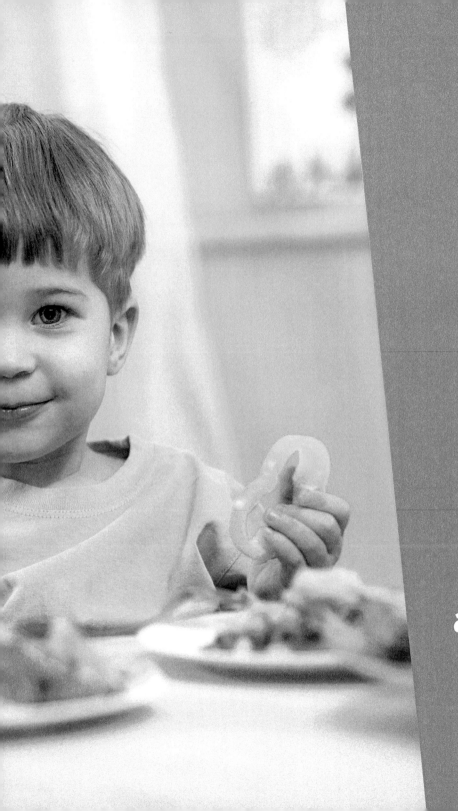

Eating a healthy diet can help build strong bones so children grow and develop well, improve concentration at school, maintain a healthy weight and help keep kids alert and active.

LET'S START EATING HEALTHY FOODS AND THEN GO OUTSIDE AND PLAY!

Made in the USA
San Bernardino, CA
18 July 2018